500

Chat-up Lines

and put downs

Stewart Ferris

SUMMERSDALE

Copyright © Summersdale Publishers 1996

Summersdale Publishers
46 West Street
Chichester
West Sussex
PO19 1RP
United Kingdom

A CIP catalogue record for this book
is available from the British Library.

Printed and bound in Great Britain by Selwood Printing Ltd.

ISBN 1 873475 78 0

Cartoons by Ellis Nadler

Acknowledgements

Thanks to Jasmine Birtles, Amy Mandeville and Alastair Williams,
all experts in this genre.

Do you think you could fall for me?
Only if you pushed me.

Shall we go and see a film?
I've seen it.

Do you fancy coming for a walk in the woods?
What for — to meet your family?

I want people to like me for what I am.
Is that why you drive a Porsche?

Can you give me your name, please?
I don't think 'Melissa' would suit you.

Do you believe in sex before marriage?
In general, yes, but with you I'd make an exception.

What's your favourite film?
Kodak.

What's the biggest problem in your life?
Look in a mirror.

What's your favourite record?
Sebastion Coe's 1500 metres.

I'd like to take you to dinner.
Sure — can you pick me up again afterwards?

When will we meet again?
In another life, I hope.

What would you say is my best feature?
Your ornamental pond.

Will you sleep with me.
No, I'm an insomniac.

Is that your face or has your neck just been sick?
Is that stain meant to be there or have you wet yourself?

I'm a photographer for a model agency:
I've been looking for a face like yours.
I'm a plastic surgeon.
I've been looking for a face like yours.

Where are you from?
Here.
I like the way you've decorated this pub.

Read my palm. What does it tell you?
That you're a train spotter.

Are you a miner?
No.
Oh, so that's not a pickaxe in your pocket?

How would you like your
eggs in the morning?

Unfertilised, mate. Piss off.

Are you separated?
No, it's just the way I walk.

Do you know what I am?
A eunuch?

Would you like my ship to sail into your port?
No. It's an airport.

Can I drive my train into your tunnel?
Sorry, I don't take express trains.

If I could dance, I'd ask you to dance, but I can't.
If I could sail, I'd take you sailing, but I can't.
However, I'm the father of twelve kids. How about it?

Let me introduce myself: I'm your future husband. If you
don't believe it I'll show you my crystal ball.

Where would you recommend round here?
The VD clinic.

I work in the music business.
I know, I've been to your shop.

Kiss me and I'll tell you a secret.
I know your secret - I work at the clinic.

How do you keep an idiot in suspense?
Don't know.
Nor me. Been waiting for someone to tell me, actually.

Can I have your autograph? I'm a huge fan.
I'd say gross.

Can you buy me a drink?
Probably. I'll check with my accountant next week.

Can you spare us the price of a cup of coffee, miss?
Not sure. Can I take your fax number and get back to you?

I'm a weight-lifter.
You look more like a shirt-lifter.

I like your teeth: perfect for stripping wallpaper.

Can you see me in your future?

No. You're already in my past.

Didn't I see your face in a medical research journal?
No, but yours may soon be.

Are you a local?
Yes.
OK, I'll talk more slowly.

Nice clothes. Do they still make them?

Is that a friend of yours or are you a social worker?

What do you think of Shirley Bassey?
I don't normally think of her, actually.

I'm a doctor: what's your appendix doing tonight? I'd love to take it out.

Very funny. You should be on the television — then I could turn you off.

Great shirt - I've seen it in the shops.
I didn't think anyone would buy it.
It needed a foster home.

Good evening. I've never had alcohol before,
but I'm feeling adventurous tonight.

Hop on for the ride of your life!
What is it — ghost train?

I like the way you dye your roots brown.
At least I've got roots.

What happened to your face? Is there anything I can do?
Not as far as I can tell, no.

Is there enough alcohol in this pub
for you to want to sleep with me?

Don't they sell make-up where you come from?

Hello? Is there anyone behind the make-up?

Hello — I'm married, but this is a business trip.

Hi. I sell safety glass. I could get you a
toughened make-up mirror if you like.

It's nice to see you off the streets for a change.

I'm fat, I'm ugly, I'm hairy, I'm smelly, and I fart like a
wind tunnel. But I'm bloody rich.
*I don't want you thinking I'm just after your money,
darling. What's your name?*

What are you doing here? Is the strip club closed tonight?

Bet you can't write your name in the snow when you piss.

Hi, I really like your laugh. You should work
on a ghost train ride.
You should be in it.

I've forgotten your name but I'll never forget your face. I'm reminded of it every morning when I hop on the back of the bus.
Why would you hop on a bus? Wouldn't it be easier to use both legs?

I like your body. How much did it cost?
You'll never afford it.

Did you know that men with the smallest dicks
have the **biggest mouths?** (Close your mouth tightly).
I could park my car in your mouth.

Are you alright?
Not any more.

Bloody hell, watch where you're going!
(As she bumps into you. You can then apologise
and offer to make it up to her with a drink later.)

Can I buy you a drink?
I would think so — why don't you ask the barman?

Can you microwave this?
Yes, but it will be too hot to wear afterwards.

Could you help me with my bag, please?
Sure. Where is she?

Didn't I see you here before?
Yes, just now.

Every time I come here I've seen you.
I'd like to know more about you.
So would the police.

Everyone says you were in the local paper this week
. . . is this true? Tell me about it.
It's not true. It was the week before.

Got a light?
Yes thanks.

Hello.
Goodbye.

Have you got a problem with that?
No, only with you.

Hey, we've met before, haven't we?
No, officer.

I don't suppose you would be interested in going
out one night to see a film?
I'm already booked that night.

Jingle bells, jingle bells . . .
(You're bound to meet someone if you go carol singing.)
What are you doing? It's June.

Isn't it boring here? Do you want to go somewhere else?
You go — that will be enough to liven things up.

37

I don't normally do this sort of thing, but here's my card —
I'd like too meet you some time.
You just did.

Keep it up — you're doing well.
I wish I could say the same for you.

Life has been
empty without you.

*I'm not letting
you fill me up.*

Kiss me.
You'll have to drug me first.

Let me help you with your shopping.
I've already done my shopping. I'm just having trouble getting it home.

I love your hair.
Which one?

Mine's a gin and tonic.
That explains the obvious dampness.

Nobody I know can tell me who you are,
but I'm sure I've seen you before.
Why don't you take that ugly mask off so that I
can see what you look like?

No, don't tell me: you're a Pisces?
OK, I won't tell you.

Ooh, you don't wanna do that.
Hmm.

Perhaps I've said this to you before, I can't remember, but you've got beautiful eyes. Probably.

I forgot my phone number, can I borrow yours?

Please take a seat.
Where to?

How did you get to be so beautiful?
I must have been given your share.

Ring me sometime. Must dash now, but here's my number.
Don't you have a name?

Shall we share a taxi to the nightclub?
I wouldn't even share the earth with you if I had a choice.

Queuing is so boring, don't you find?

It is now.

Shall we introduce ourselves?
I already know myself. What about you?

You'd look good in anything but the mirror.
At least I've got a mirror.

There's a party tonight. Do you want to come?
You wouldn't get in. I'm going on my own.

Tell me about yourself - you look interesting.
You look like you model for death threats.

What do you think of the music here?
Better than the company.

Umpteen people must have already told you this,
but you're very beautiful.
You're so ugly, Frankenstein's Monster would go to a
Halloween party as you.

What would you do if you ever
got chatted-up by a woman?

Warn her that I
used to be one.

Virtually everyone here is ugly except you.
*Well you're so ugly I bet your psychiatrist makes you lie face
down on the couch.*

Very difficult getting served here. What are you having in
case I get served first?
An attack of nausea.

Weren't you at the party last week?
Yes. And I haven't changed my mind since then, I'm afraid.

Where is the toilet?
Oh, I didn't realise you were house trained.

You show me yours, I'll show you mine.
OK, my boyfriend's over there.

Do you take the washing-up out of the sink
before you piss into it?
No. Nor after.

Feel a muscle, any muscle.
All these curves, and me with no brakes.

Zoos are morally unacceptable, don't you think?
(If she is standing near a zoo holding a protest placard.)

Can I borrow your phone?
Why?
My ex told me to call when I fell in love again.

Can I borrow ten pence? I want to call my
mother and thank her.
I'd complain if I were you.

Can I have directions?
To where?
To your heart.

Do you know where we are?
Why?
Because I'm lost in your eyes.

Do you have the number for heaven?
Why?
It looks like they've lost an angel.

Do you know what would look good on you?
No?
Me.

Going my way? Can I walk with you?
You can walk near me.

How about I sit on your lap and we'll see what pops up?

(Put a little water on him/her)
How about you and I go back to my place
and get out of these wet clothes?

Hi, shy guy. Someone once told me that the loneliest people
on this earth are shy men and beautiful women. I thought I'd
come over and put both of us out of our misery.

If I had created the alphabet I would
have put 'U' and 'I' together.

Is your daddy a thief?
No.
Then how did he steal the stars
out of the sky and put them in your eyes?

Is your daddy a thief?
Yes.
Can he get me a cheap video?

I've never chatted anybody up before. Will you teach me?

I miss my teddy bear. Will you sleep with me?
Here, borrow mine.

I want you to melt in my mouth, not in my hand.

I have been watching you dance. It occurred to me since neither of us can dance, maybe we could just sit down and have a drink.

(Look at his shirt label. When they say 'What are you doing':)
Just checking to see if you're my size
OR
Just checking to see if you were made in heaven.

Let's go to my place and do all the things
I'll tell everyone we did anyway.

Let's play Hillbillies. You be my brother and we'll inbreed.

Shall I tell you my name?
Why?
So you'll know what to scream.

May I have a drag on your fag?
That's ironic — actually I am a fag in drag.

Let's skip the awkward beginning and pretend that we have known each other for a while. So, how's your Mum?

She told me I wasn't to see you any more.

Nice hat. Can I have it?

Please talk to me so that creep over
there will leave me alone.
I just said that to someone about you.

Nice tie. It matches my duvet.

Nice shoes. Take me.

(Grab his/her bum) **Pardon me, is this seat taken?**

The word of the day is 'legs'. Let's go back to
my place and spread the word.

That outfit would look great in a crumpled heap on my
bedroom floor.

Would you be my love buffet, so I can lay you out on the
table and take what I want?
Sorry, salami's off today.

Weren't you in Paris in the summer of '93?
No, I was there in the riots of '68.

Will you let me buy you a drink? Or at least walk me to the bar. I left my glasses at home and am completely blind.

Will you marry me?

You're lovelier than my fleas.

Your daddy must have been a baker, 'cause you sure have a nice set of buns.

You look happy. Have you just farted?

If you can't stand the beat, get off the dancefloor.
No, it's just you I can't stand.

You look likely. Want to take a shower with me?

Did anyone ever tell you how beautiful you are
— and mean it?

I'm not interested in a relationship, but I don't feel like being alone tonight.

Are you asking for a shag, or what?

Zabaglione is my favourite dessert. If you're nice you can come home with me for a taste.

What's your best way of avoiding the morning rush hour in town?
I stay in bed.

How old do you think I am?
Why don't you ask your teacher that question?

I'm an expert at chat-up techniques. Would you like lessons?
I might be tempted to play truant.

Sorry I can't think straight — my mind's on your curves.

Close your eyes, hold out your hands, and I'll put something nice in them.

Excuse me, I'm a stranger here.
Can you direct me to your house?
I don't need any more staff right now. Sorry.

I'm a sculptor. Will you model for me?
Why?
I've been commissioned to make a statue of a pig.

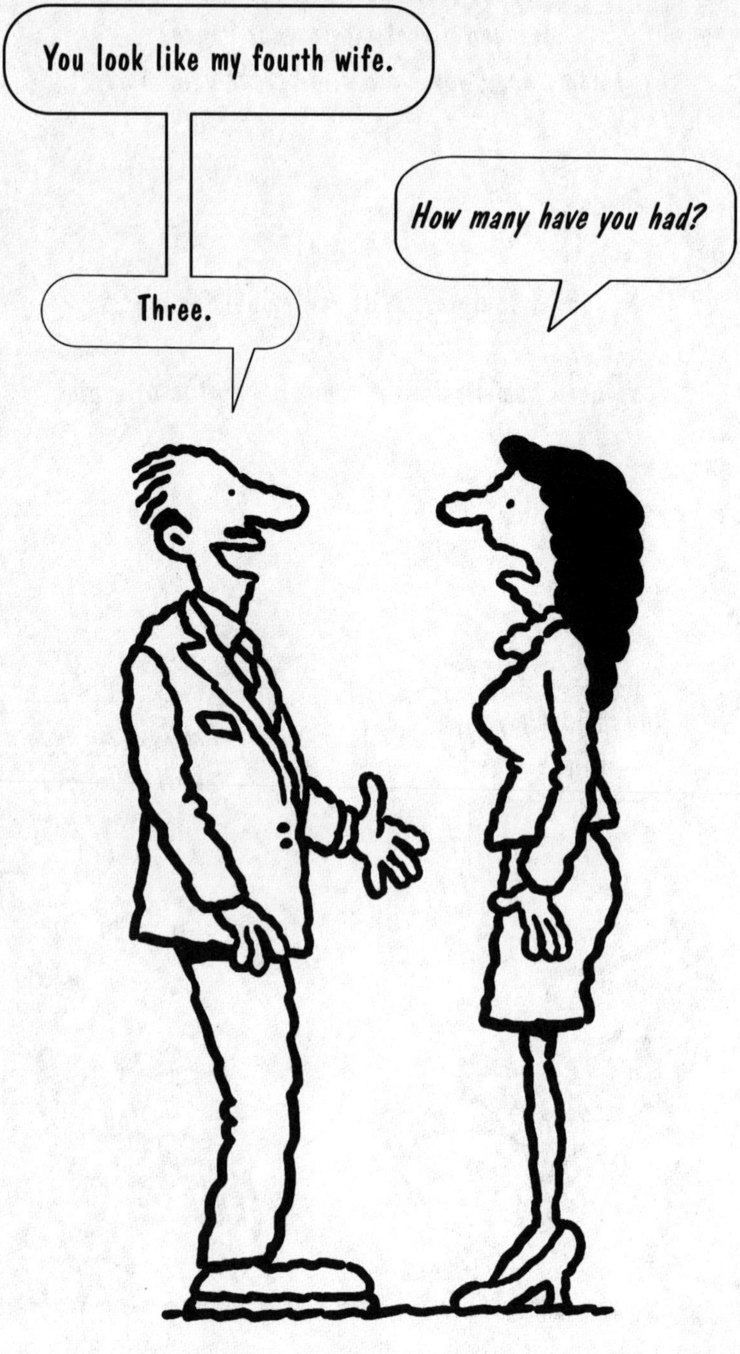
You look like my fourth wife.
How many have you had?
Three.

Would you like to improve your image? Be seen with me.

Tell me about yourself: your pains,
your dreams, your phone number.

Can I have your phone number?
No, but you can have my dialling code.

Would you mind if I take a lock of your hair?
Why, are you trying to stuff a mattress?

Are you married?
No, just practising.

Your smile could ripen bananas.
Have you got one we could try it on?

You've got everything a man could want:
teeth, hair, moustache . . .
All I lack is your charm and subtlety.

You're the kind of girl I'd like to take home to mother except I can't trust my father.

Don't worry — he's not the sort to drink from the same cup twice.

Your face must turn a few heads.
Yours must turn a few stomachs.

You look like a million dollars — all green and wrinkled.

You've got romantic eyes — I can tell by the way they
snuggle up to each other.

With a face like yours you
should be in radio.

*Have you ever considered
deep sea diving?
Without oxygen?*

Your face is familiar — I might even say commonplace.
Yours must have been a limited edition — limited because
no one else wanted one like it.

Hi, I'm a millionaire.
Lire doesn't count.

What happened to your face?
Do you step on rakes for a hobby?
No, I impersonate you.

Brains aren't everything, but in your case they're nothing.
I don't understand.

I don't know what makes you so stupid,
but whatever it is, it works.
I studied hard for it.

I'm pleased to tell you that we've held a
competition and you've won my heart.
First prize and booby prize all rolled into one.

I'd like to show you the world.
Is that it under your jumper?

I'm raising money for charity by charging for kisses.
Never mind the kisses, just take the money.

Are you sisters?
Yes.
You must have left Cinderella at home.

When will we meet again?
Beats me.

I've just painted my bedroom ceiling.
Would you like to come and look at it?
*I'm about to throw up, so if you don't mind me decorating
the floor at the same time . . .*

I'm a vegetarian.
Do you love animals?
No, I hate vegetables.

I can read you like a book.
Great — let's get straight to the last chapter.

You don't sweat much for a fat lass.
I will when I start running away from you.

I had no idea I would ever
meet someone like you in here.

*I had no idea they would
ever **let** someone like
you in here.*

Would you massage my body?
No, I'm an accountant. I can only massage your figures.

I'd like to see you.
Well open your eyes.

I'd like to see you again.
Certainly. I'll send you a photo.

I'd like to visit your inner temple and
worship your womanhood.
You have to take your shoes off before you come in.

Give me a smile and I'll give you the world.
You got anything smaller?

Would you like to have a pizza with me?
A piece of what?

What do you think of me?
I don't think of you . . . ever!

I'd paint the Forth Bridge for you.
OK. See you in seven years when you've finished it.

If I said you had a beautiful body
would you hold it against me?
*If I told you what you looked like would you crawl back under
your rock?*

Are you a model?
Yes, but you're not a working model.

Hey, you're not much of a looker, but I'll have you.

Thanks. You must be very open-minded. Was that how your brain slipped out?

Get your coat love, you've pulled.
If I want your opinion I'll give it to you.

Oi, darling, do you want to really enjoy yourself?
*If I wanted to enjoy myself I wouldn't be
standing here talking to you.*

I'm a real lady-killer.
Yes, after one night with you they probably commit suicide.

Hey, babe, couldn't you just go for me?
Why, can't you go for yourself?

I've got the body of a fighter.
Isn't he annoyed about that?

I've got something that makes girls go mad.
What, rabies?

You're very pretty, but your eyes indicate you've had a sheltered life.

They've only been sheltering from you.

If you give me a chance I'll grow on you.
Yeh, like a verruca.

Do you come here often?
No, but now I know you do I won't bother coming at all.

I've got some condoms, so I think we should sleep together right now.

What's the hurry? Are they close to their expiry date?

That's a great dress, but it would look better
on my bedroom floor.
No, there wouldn't be room with all your two year old pants.

Do you have a licence for those mammaries, madam?
Yes, but I'm not showing you.

I bet you could light up the whole room when you smile.
(SHE SMILES)
I was wrong.

Do you always wear an industrial corset?
No, sometimes I wear a sports model.

Listen, I've been wanting to tell you how I feel for months, but the right opportunity never seemed to arise. I always look out for you when I come here, and you brighten up my day whenever I see you. I just want to tell you that you're the most beautiful woman I've ever seen. I love you.
Good morning, sir. Can I help you?

Are you into athletics?
I did the high jump when I saw your face.

Is there anything I can do for you?
*I doubt it. There was obviously nothing you could
do for yourself.*

I'd like to sit with someone beautiful, charming and witty.
So would I, but no one here fits that description.

Weren't you going round with a friend of mine recently?
Yes, we met in a revolving door.

Aren't you the blonde girl I saw here on Friday?
No, I'm the brunette you saw here on Thursday.

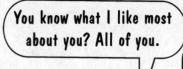

I'd like to go out with you,
but I'm getting married tomorrow.
How about next week, then?

Are you married?
No, I'm happily divorced.

I'd like to take you fishing.
Great, you can provide the worm.

I'm sure I could turn you on.
You couldn't even turn on a radio.

Would you like to join me?
Why, are you falling apart?

You'll have to forgive me if I yawn, only I'm a bit tired.

Yes, you look exhausted. Have you been feeling yourself?

I'm not well. I haven't been feeling myself lately.
Would you like to feel me instead?

I like a girl who's nice to cuddle.
So do I.

I'm not myself tonight.
Yes, I've noticed an improvement.

What's your problem? Did you wake up grumpy this morning?
No, I let him sleep.

Can I kiss you?
Of course, but mind you don't burn yourself on my cigarette.

Don't you think I look like Tom Cruise?
Yes, but I've heard your undercarriage looks like Tom Thumb's.

How did you get that scar on your arm?
Probably in the same way that you got your face.

I've been working out in the gym. What do you think of my condition?
Unpleasant, but stable.

Where did you get that facelift?
The same place you got that penis extension.
What, the balloon pump shop?

Where can we go from here?
I don't care, so long as you go first.

Can I have your name?

Why — haven't you already got one?

Where can I find love?
At the beginning of a tennis match.

My stars said I would meet the woman of my dreams tonight.
I'll go and see if I can find her for you.

Tell me your star sign.

Virgo. Intactus.

Is it true that you're a famous cook?
You must have misheard. I rob banks for a living.

I work in motor racing. I'm a test driver.
Yeh, for Scalextric.

I'm a wine taster.
Shame you have no taste in clothes, though.

I'm the man you've been looking for.
What, the pest control officer?

I want to die in your arms.
Sure, what colour?

I'm considering chucking my girlfriend for you. How do you feel about that?

But I don't want your girlfriend.

You're so lovely I'd like to drink your bathwater.
I think you'd probably end up eating your words as well.

Tell me a secret about yourself.
I've slept with everyone in this bar, apart from you, and
every one has been better than the last. I'd hate to carry on
and be disappointed, so I've stopped.

I've heard you're a good cook, but there is
no recipe for my love for you.
What about Mini Sausages with Leeks?

What would you like for breakfast tomorrow?
*Actually I didn't think you had the capability of working up
an appetite in me. Maybe just a slice of toast. No butter.*

What's your favourite food?
Ground rhino horn.

Would you like some coq au vin?
What sort of van do you drive?

When I roll across my satin sheets at night, the sound reminds me of you.

What, while I'm eating a packet of crisps?

If I had known I was going to meet someone as amazingly
lovely as you, I'd have had my nostrils plucked.
And if I'd known I was going to meet someone as ugly as
you, I'd have had my eyeballs plucked.

Am I ever in your dreams?
No, only in my nightmares.

I'm afraid I'm an incurable romantic.
Well, you're incurable, that's for sure.

I've waited all my life to meet you.
Stuck at the back of the queue, were you?

No one makes me feel like you do.
You must have caught my cold.

May I introduce myself?
Certainly — try those people over there.

I think I've seen you before. Have we studied together?
Yes, at the dog obedience classes. You failed, as I recall.

What brings you to this neck of the woods?
My car.

My friends told me all about you.
What friends?

Don't you think that a man's charisma is more important than the size of his penis?

But you've got hardly any charisma either.

What line of work are you in?
Double yellow lines. I'm a traffic warden.

Did you get dressed in the dark, by any chance?
Did you cut your hair yourself?

Is your diet not going too well, then?
It's going as badly as your chat-up technique.

Would it have helped if you had worn a bra during your formative years?

Maybe. It obviously worked for you.

You seem to drink a lot. I think you need help.
No, no, I can drink it all by myself.

Shall we go beachcombing?
*I think you should start with your hair and work up to
beaches when you've got the hang of it.*

I'm feeling a bit depressed. Have you got any advice?
Yes, bloody cheer up.

I'm looking for my future wife.
I think she's over there with your ex-wife.

Do you think I look cool?
I'm not sure, but your loins appear to be
suffering from the cold.

Fancy a roll in the hay?
No, just a sandwich.

You remind me of my favourite Disney character
— Snow White.
You too — the Hunchback of Notre Dame.

Would you like to come and see my stamp collection?
I've seen it — it's on that envelope in your pocket.

My ancestors died in the Wars of the Roses.
Must have been a serious flower competition.

124

The pillar outside this building symbolises my feelings for you.
You've just trod in the stuff that symbolises my feelings for you.

I bet you couldn't chat me up if you tried.
Good. I won't bother then.

I love your nose. Can I join you?
No. Did you enjoy that?

Don't go away — I'm just going to put the kettle on.
Are you sure it will fit you?

More tea, vicar?
I'm not that sort of man, actually.

Do you like getting to know strangers for the first time?
I used to.

I'm Frank, so you can rely on me to speak my mind.
That shouldn't take long.

My name's Russell — you can hear me coming.
I'm Ivy — but I don't think I'll grow on you.

Hi. My name's Andrew.
Oh, I'd have thought you were an Andrea.

The name's Thomas,
John Thomas.

*That's OK, I'm Holly, so
I'm used to little pricks.*

My name's June, but you can call me April.
May I?

If I wrote a poem about my passion for you,
would you display it?
Yes — to the judge, to help me get an injunction on you.

I find it hard to articulate my feelings for you.
That's OK — part of you is speaking for itself.

You're lucky we met. People like me don't
grow on trees, you know.
No, they usually swing from them.

Stick with me, and I'll get you on TV.
Will you catch me if I fall off?

I saw your face in the reflection of the moonlight
on the lake last night.
No you didn't.

You have a classical look. It reminds me of a
bust I saw recently.
In a gallery?
No, a magazine.

I'm only as old as the woman I feel.
So you're about six?

I've just finished my studies. Do you want to
celebrate with me?
No, I'm with a team of scientists. We're still studying you.

Did you hear the request I put in for you on the radio?
Oh, was it two pints of beer and a packet of crisps?

If you should happen to
fall in love with me, I'll be
waiting for you.

If I ever get that
desperate I won't be
worth waiting for.

I don't know who you are, but I really feel
something for you.
Well stop feeling it in public.

You would be in my final thoughts if I were to be
run over by a bus.
That's because I'd be driving it.

If I were a policeman I'd arrest you and interrogate you for hours, just the two of us, naked on top of the freezer in my garage, listening to Abba songs.
Right, you're nicked you sick pervert.

Let me buy you a drink — I've just been promoted.
You're allowed to serve fries now?

I'm a boxer, and there's a big fight tomorrow,
so you needn't worry about me trying to sleep with you
'cos my trainer won't allow it.
Jealous type, is he?

I like girls who wear uniforms.
How about me — I work at McDonald's.

Will you join me
in a glass of wine?

*I don't think there'd be
room for both of us.*

I like tough, brave women.
Is that why you're married to a Lollypop lady?

You remind me of my pet cat, warm and fluffy.
You remind me of my pet worm, small and slimy.

Do you want to dance with me?
No, I'm not wearing my steel toe capped boots.

Inside this exquisite body there's an exquisite
personality trying to get out.
Could have fooled me.

I never forget a face.

Neither do I, but in your case I'll make an exception.

Can I introduce you to my dog, Raffles?
Oh, isn't he big? Can I stroke him?
Of course. Would you like to stroke Raffles as well?

God ordered me to come to you.
What's He up to? That's the fifth one this week.
I've sent all the others back.

I've come from another planet to seek out
beautiful life forms.
Is that because your race is so ugly?

I want people to love me for myself, not my money.
Isn't that narrowing your options somewhat?

You look like you're suffering from a severe case of virginity.
Yeh, and it looks like it's catching.

Would you like to come and see my garden? I've been working
hard at it, and now it looks beautiful.
*Shame you couldn't put the same amount of
effort into your face.*

How deeply do you feel for me?
About sewer level.

I'd do anything for you.
Alright, make yourself handsome.

Shall we do it on my waterbed?
That would be like a jumbo jet trying to land on a mirror dinghy. Not a good idea.

Do you fancy going halves on a bastard?
How? Are you going to split yourself down the middle?

I love your crazy hair — it looks like you've got grass growing out of it.

That's odd — I planted tulips.

What would you give me if I agreed to sleep with you?
Syphilis?

I've seen you working in the bakery. Why do you
work such long hours?
I knead the dough.

I've just been to the doctor. I thought I had acute angina, but he said I was imagining it.

No, no, he's wrong — it's gorgeous.

You're the best looking bloke I've ever seen.
Thanks, I wish I could say the same for you.
You could if you were as big a liar as me.

Am I the first person who has ever tried to seduce you?
You could be — your face looks familiar.

Your dribble reminds me of a country stream.
Your face reminds me of the sea — it makes me sick.

Why don't you look me up sometime?
I can't — I haven't got a directory of reptiles.

I'm always being pressured towards marriage, actually.
Who by — your parents?

My ideal woman has to have a great sense of humour.
That will have to be the only sense she has.

Do you mind if I sit on your knee?
What's wrong with your high chair?

I've always believed in love at first sight.

So did I — until I met you.

I'm researching a book of favourite chat-up lines.
What's yours?
A lager, please.

Would you like to improve the quality of your bloodline?
You've got less pedigree than a tin of Chum.

On the way here I had a premonition that we would be
destined to meet here tonight.
Well I do work here, after all.

It's OK, we can be together tonight. I've given my girlfriend the evening off.

What for, good behaviour?

Show me the way to your heart.
It's via your wallet.

Were your parents aliens, or did you have an
accident with a cement mixer?
*No, my face did this as an expression of sympathy and
solidarity when it saw yours.*

What's your favourite museum?
Yorkshire.

If you were a fish, I'd be your chip.
Yeh, limp and soggy.

Was your dad a carpenter, 'cos I *wooden* half love
to *screw* you.
He's over there, so why don't you ask him?
If you were a computer, I'd give you some pretty exciting

software on a disk.
A floppy one, I presume?

Which lake would you most like to visit?
The EU wine lake.

Would you like a ride on my love missile?
Love missile? Love pea-shooter, more like.

Hi there. I'd like to ask you what's your idea of a perfect evening?

The one I was having before you came over.

I find you strangely appealing.
I just find you strange.

Am I everything you thought I'd be?
Yes, everything and worse.

Do you have a favourite singer?

Yes, the ones with two bobbins and a foot pedal.

Welsh Chat-up Lines:

Would you like a drink?
Baaaa.

I like a girl who wears real wool.
Baaaa.

I'd like to take you out to eat.
What's your favourite field?
Baaaa.

Scouse chat-up lines:

Do you want to have a ride in my car?
OK. What have you got?
Dunno — let's have a look in the car park
and see what we like.

Scottish chat-up lines:

Can I buy you a drink?
No.
Great. Let's just talk instead.

Eton chat-up lines:

Hi. I'm new here.
Bend over, then.

London chat-up lines:

Gor blimey, 'ow about a skating rink me ol' apple and banana?
Yes please. With ice and lemon.

What would I have to give you to get a little kiss?

Chloroform.

French chat-up lines:

Puis j'utilise ton boite de lettres?

C'est une grande baguette dans ta poche? Ou est-ce qu'il te fait plaisir a me voir?

Un royal cheese et un coca. Avec glacons. Et un bisou, s'il vous plait.

Ma verge est plus grande que le Tour Eiffel.

T'es plus jolie que mon couchon.

T'as les plus grandes poitrines que j'ai jamais vu.

Ooh la la.

Tu n'est pas aussi laide dans le soleil.

Je voudrais etre ton mec. Ca fait combien?

American chat-up lines:

Gee. (sic)

Say, you're real neat. (sic)

Do you wanna see a movie with me? (sic)

By the same author:

HOW TO
CHAT-UP
WOMEN

STEWART FERRIS

£4.99

Also available: **How To Chat-up Men**
Amy Mandeville
£4.99

How To Stay Married
Dick Hills
£4.99